The
YAWARA STICK
and
POLICE BATON

The YAWARA STICK
and POLICE BATON

By

J. McCauslin Moynahan, Jr.

Second Degree Black Belt, Okazaki Ju Jitsu
Shodan (First Degree Black Belt), Shudokan Karate
1k Kyu (First Degree Brown Belt), Kodokan Judo

Pullman, Washington

Original publication 1963
Reprint 2024
Budoworks Publishing
All rights reserved

ACKNOWLEDGMENTS

The author wishes to thank the following individuals for their help in the preparation of this text: Mr. Stephen Nelson for his photography; Mr. Victor Hall; Mr. Earl Hogge; and Patrolman Ray Pfiester. Special thanks goes to Web Ruble for his work in the proofreading of this book.

J.M.M.

Contents

I GENERAL 1

II YOU AND THE YAWARA STICK 2

III STRIKING WITH THE YAWARA STICK 6

IV VITAL AREAS 12

    Bone Edge Group 13

    Vital Point Group 14

    Nerve Release Centers 16

V YAWARA STICK "COME ALONGS" 19

    Two Fingers Come Along 21

    Four Fingers Come Along 22

    Arm Scissors Come Along 24

    Straight Arm Bar Come Along 26

    Neck Come Along 28

    Barb Come Along 29

VI YAWARA STICK ESCAPES 30

    Wrist Escape No. 1 31

    Wrist Escape No. 2 33

    One Handed Lapel 34

    Two Handed Lapel 35

    One Hand on Belt 36

    Two Hands on Belt 37

    Front Choke 38

    Rear Choke (Arms Extended) 39

    Naked Choke 40

    Bear Hug (Over Arms) 41

    Bear Hug (Under Arms) 42

    Grasp From Behind (Over Arms) 43

Grasp From Behind (Under Arms)..44

Hammer Lock 45

Head Lock 46

Full Nelson 47

Running Attack 48

Two Man Attack (Front and Back)..49

Two Man Attack (Right and Left) 50

I GENERAL...53

II HOW TO STRIKE WITH THE BATON 54

III GENERAL BATON DEFENSES 60

V BATON COME ALONGS 66

The Crotch Come Along..67

The Arm Bar Come Along 68

The Choke Come Alongs 69

Choke One Come Along 69

Choke Two Come Along..70

Choke Three Come Along 71

V MISCELLANEOUS BATON ESCAPES...................................72

The
YAWARA STICK
and
POLICE BATON

SECTION ONE
The Yawara Stick

I

GENERAL

THE YAWARA STICK as sold in many of the Police Supply houses is not very old. The idea of stick fighting is, however, very old. Stick fighting of various kinds has been known in the Orient for at least 2,000 years. Almost every Oriental country has some type of stick fighting. It is almost impossible to name the individual who created the techniques utilized with the Yawara Stick.

A gentleman named Matasuyama did the actual perfecting of the six inch, six ounce electro-plastic weapon that we now term the Yawara Stick. He is also credited with the perfecting of many of the Yawara Stick techniques. However, some of these same techniques and similar ones are based on techniques of the old Ju-Jitsu schools located in Japan. Often these Ju-Jitsu schools taught the use of a larger club or stick but most of the techniques are identical.

The staff (similar to that of Robin Hood's) was used in old China and Japan by monks to ward off attacks. These monks became very proficient in its use and application. A good staff man can do wonders against a knife fighter, boxer, judo man, etc.

Due to the fact that the historical information on the Yawara Stick type fighting is scant, to say the least, no more will be said on this topic. It should be remembered by the reader that this art is based upon the Oriental methods of stick fighting.

In the following work the author will try to omit difficult maneuvers. Long discussions on the applications of certain techniques will also be avoided wherever possible. This book is based on the assumption that one picture is worth 1,000 words.

The techniques described are thought by the author to be the most easily learned and effective techniques available.

The student may in time devise techniques on his own to use with the Yawara Stick. This especially will be easy to do with the surplus of vital areas presented. Many escape maneuvers may be used other than those demonstrated, so the student is encouraged to be creative.

II

YOU AND THE YAWARA STICK

TO GAIN THE MOST EFFECTIVE USE from the Yawara Stick it should be held properly. The barbs on the Yawara Stick should be held so that they are running parallel with your arm and hand (Fig. 1).

You should hold your hand fairly tight but not too tight. Holding too tightly will not give you the freedom of movement you need.

Don't strike at a subject with your fist while holding the Yawara Stick in your striking hand. You may damage your fist. The Yawara Stick itself is much stronger than your fist will ever be, so strike with your Yawara Stick.

Fig. 1

Fig. 2

The Yawara Stick may be concealed many places on your person. The sports coat pocket is an excellent location for its concealment (Fig. 2). Here it is easy to locate in case of trouble.

Fig. 3

The jacket pocket also conceals the Yawara Stick well. Again, it is available if needed (Fig. 3).

Fig. 4

The hip pocket, although a little harder to get at, will also readily conceal the Yawara Stick (Fig. 4).

If the possibility of trouble is imminent you may wish to carry the Yawara Stick concealed up your sleeve. From here all you have to do is shake your arm and it will fall into your hand where you can use it (Figs. 5, 6 and 7).

Fig. 5

Fig. 6

Fig. 7

Fig. 8

Fig. 9

You may hold the Yawara Stick in your hand and cross your arms and conceal it in this way (Fig. 8).

Or, since it is small, you may hold it to your side without attracting attention (Fig. 9).

The above concealment locations should be utilized whenever possible! Do not show the Yawara Stick until you are ready to use it. The psychological advantage of frightening an opponent with the Yawara Stick is not too great, since few people actually know what it is.

If, during the time you are using it, the Yawara Stick should happen to fall on the ground it is doubtful if anyone would be able to use it were they to find it.

The reader should feel confident with the knowledge he will receive from this book. Very few have gone in for the work of studying the rise of this new and effective weapon for the police officer.

III

STRIKING WITH THE YAWARA STICK

DUE TO THE CONSTRUCTION AND MANNER in which the Yawara Stick is held, a large variety of striking maneuvers can be employed. This variety of striking maneuvers in part accounts for the great effectiveness of the Yawara Stick.

The Yawara Stick is extremely hard. If you strike an opponent with force you can easily injure him permanently. Remember that the Yawara Stick is strong enough to break a brick (Fig. 10).

Fig. 10

Study and practice the following striking maneuvers. Use a variety of maneuvers in practice to prevent becoming accustomed to only a few. Remember that these are only striking positions and may be used with a variety of vital points. Again the reader is reminded that the Yawara Stick is shown in only one hand in the illustrations. Either hand, of course, can be used.

Fig. 11

You may strike your opponent a low, jamming blow with the forward end of the Yawara Stick (Fig. 11).

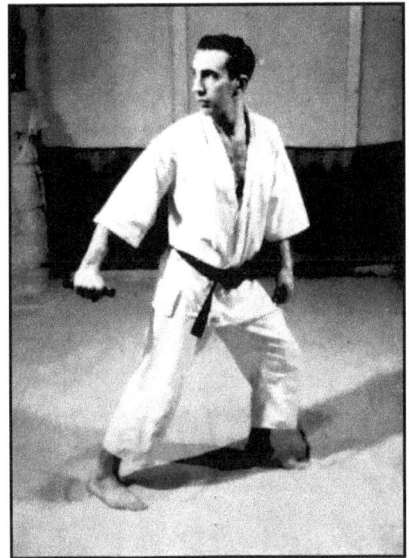

Fig. 12

If an opponent is at your rear you may make a low strike at him with the back end of the Yawara Stick (Fig. 12).

Fig. 13

You may strike an opponent who is in front of you by using a forward high strike (Fig. 13).

7

Fig. 14

The opponent who is behind you may be struck with a high backward strike (Fig. 14).

An upward blow may be utilized to develop a great deal of force (Fig. 15).

Fig. 15

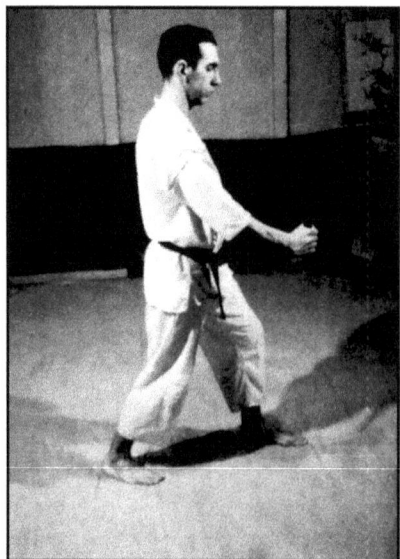

Fig. 16

A downward strike is effective against an opponent who is bending down or on the ground (Fig. 16).

8

Fig. 17

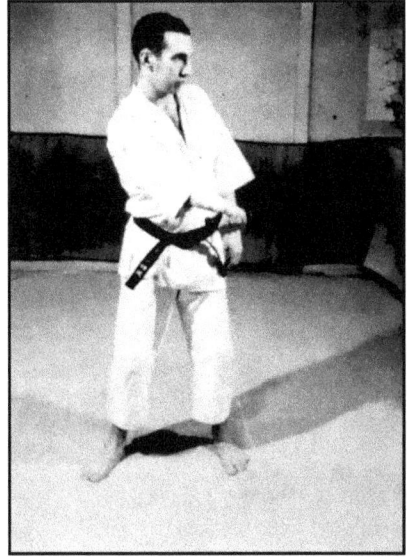
Fig. 18

For the opponent standing on your right or left, a side blow may be used (Figs. 17 and 18).

You may also strike an opponent on either your right or left side by simply turning your hand over from the position demonstrated in Figures 17 and 18. If your hand were now open the palm would be facing downward (Figs. 19 and 20).

Fig. 19

Fig. 20

9

Fig. 21

Fig. 22

You may strike the higher vital points to either your right or left by turning your hand outward and striking from side to side (Figs. 21 and 22).

Fig. 23

Fig. 24

These higher vital points may also be struck by turning your hand inward and striking to the right or left (Figs. 23 and 24).

The last striking technique to be covered is the "flicking" technique. Here you raise the Yawara Stick up and then strike with the tip of it. Just as you strike you pull the Yawara Stick back; thus your opponent receives a flicking action (Figs. 25 and 26).

Fig. 25

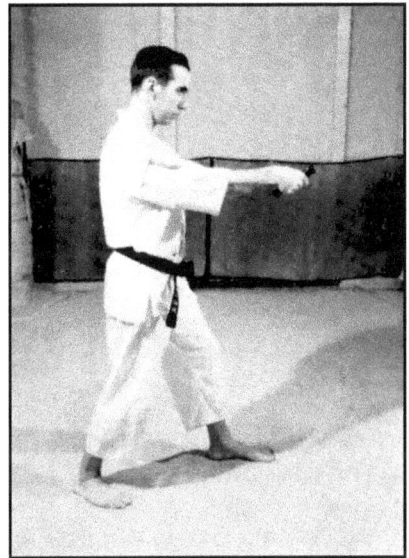

Fig. 26

IV

VITAL AREAS

THE VITAL AREAS which can be struck with the Yawara Stick are many. For our study they will be divided into three groups.

— The first group we shall call bone edges. These areas are any location on the body where the bones are not protected by muscle.

— The second group is classified as vital points. These consist of striking against muscle, organs and general weak points on the body.

— The last group is called nerve release points. Here a slight pressure is employed by the Yawara Stick to an area which is extremely sensitive.

The student is here advised not to try and learn all of the points under this section. He will do well to merely learn a few from each group. Many points are given in each group but the student is not expected to remember them all. Good knowledge of a few points is worth much more than a little knowledge of many.

Bone Edge Group

The bone edge group consists of those areas shown on the Bone Edge Diagram I. The author has omitted listing each point since the diagram is self explanatory. Some general points to remember when using the bone edge group are:

1. The harder you strike your opponent the more drastic will be the results.

2. The whole head and face area should be considered bone edges. Strike this area with care.

3. The back bone is a bone edge and extreme care also should be exercised in striking here.

4. All areas where the bones are near the surface can be classified as bone edge areas. Only the best are listed here.

5. Very little striking force is needed against a bone area to gain release from a hold.

6. Practice with care on an opponent. Don't hit your opponent on a bone edge in practice. Draw your strike just short of contact.

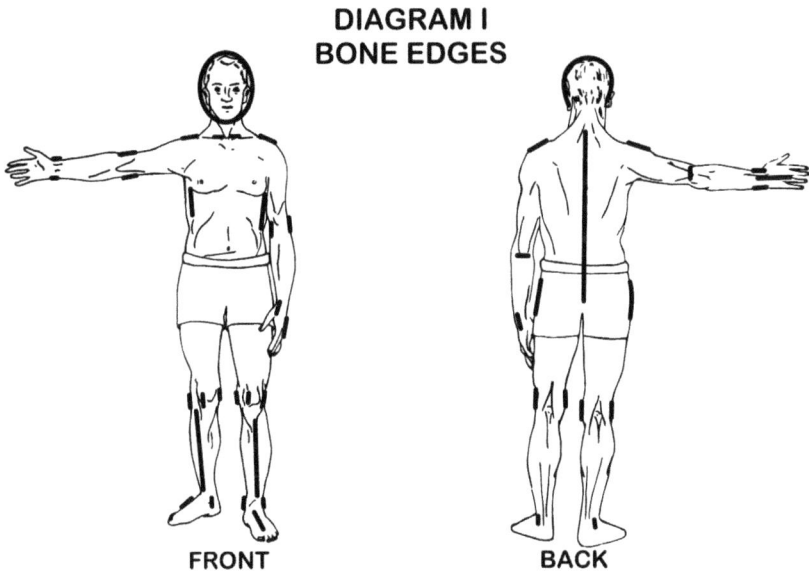

DIAGRAM I
BONE EDGES

FRONT   BACK

13

Vital Point Group

The vital point group shown on the Vital Points Diagram II consists of weak places on the body which, when struck, cause considerable pain or unconsciousness.

1. Side of neck—When struck with a reasonable amount of force the subject may be knocked out. If small force is used a stunning sensation is felt and the hold is released rapidly.

2. Neck muscles—When these muscles are struck a stunning or temporary paralysis may be felt in the shoulder and arm area.

3. Adam's apple—This area is very sensitive. Extreme caution should be used when striking this area. Unconsciousness and possibly death may result from a direct hard blow. A stunning sensation may be felt with a light to medium blow.

4. Stomach—Any location in the stomach will develop pain when a hard blow is delivered. Generally a blow will cause severe pain with the possibility of unconsciousness.

5. Kidney—Striking this area is extremely good for knocking a man down or out. A medium blow in this area will drop a man to his knees and may possibly knock him out.

6. Crotch—If sufficient force is applied you might knock a man out by a blow to the crotch. Severe pain is present when a light blow is administered.

7. Thigh muscles—A direct blow on the thigh muscles will cause pain and cramping.

8. Calf muscles—A direct blow delivered here will cause pain and cramping.

DIAGRAM II
VITAL POINTS

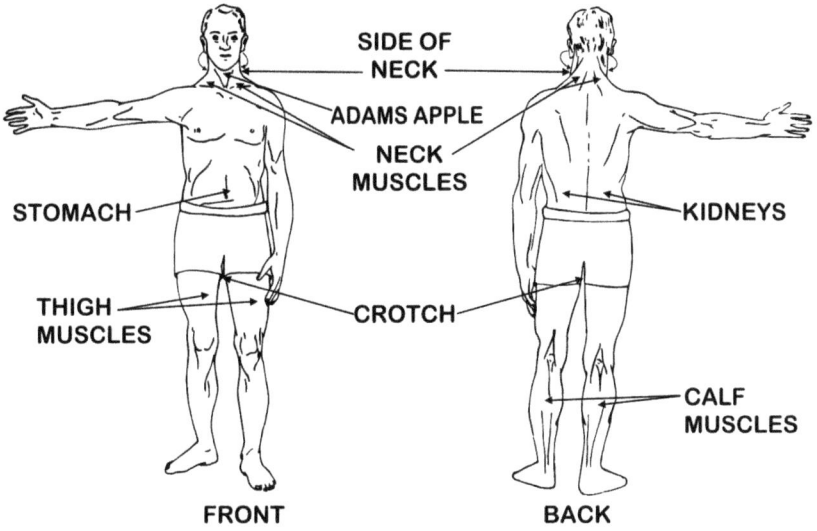

SIDE OF NECK

ADAMS APPLE

NECK MUSCLES

STOMACH

KIDNEYS

THIGH MUSCLES

CROTCH

CALF MUSCLES

FRONT

BACK

Nerve Release Centers

The nerve release centers should be utilized only when a temporary escape is necessary. The results of pressure against these areas is merely temporary pain or discomfort. The force exerted will be either direct pressure with the end of the Yawara Stick or pressure with the barb of the Yawara Stick. These points will best be utilized while someone is holding you. *See Nerve Release Diagram III.*

1. Eyes—Pressure should be exerted with the end of the Yawara Stick in a forward manner against your opponent's eye. This is not a striking move; rather you place the end of the Yawara Stick against his eye and push.

2. Bridge of nose—Place the barb against the bridge of the nose and push forward.

3. Under the ears—Place the end of the Yawara Stick against the edge of the jaw under the ear and push inward and upward.

4. Adam's apple—Place the end of the Yawara Stick against the Adam's apple and push forward.

5. Pit of throat—The end of the Yawara Stick should be placed against the hollow spot below the Adam's apple known as the pit. A forward and downward force should be exerted.

6. Ribs—Place the end of the Yawara Stick between any two ribs and with a twisting motion push forward.

7. Radius bone—Put the barb near where the radius bone and hand meet and press against the bone.

8. Back of wrists—Place the end of the Yawara Stick against the tendons on the back of the hand and drag or pull the Yawara Stick back and forth across them.

9. Finger joints—Put the barb on any of the joints and apply pressure.

10. Top of feet—Place the end of the Yawara Stick against the tendons and pull the Yawara Stick back and forth across them.

DIAGRAM III
NERVE RELEASE CENTERS

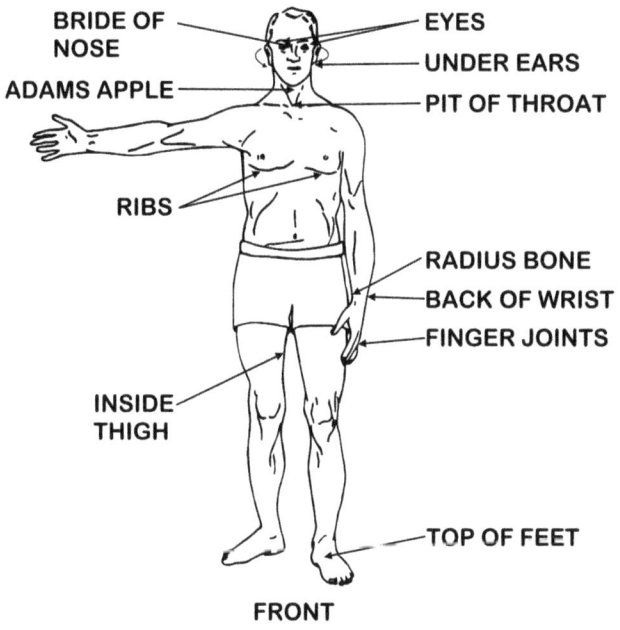

BRIDE OF NOSE

EYES

ADAMS APPLE

UNDER EARS

PIT OF THROAT

RIBS

RADIUS BONE

BACK OF WRIST

FINGER JOINTS

INSIDE THIGH

TOP OF FEET

FRONT

V

YAWARA STICK "COME ALONGS"

THE FOLLOWING "COME ALONGS" are but a few of those which can be applied when using the Yawara Stick. The essentials of a good come along are speed, timing, surprise, practice, and knowledge of the come along. With all of these elements a come along can be executed with a maximum of efficiency.

Speed is a must, in order for a come along to work. Without speed a subject can easily protect himself from the application of a technique. Speed is therefore an extremely important part in the application of a come along.

Timing is another element which must be correct. Just as everything in an automobile engine must work in harmony to perform properly, so must everything work in a come along technique. This is what is called timing—everything working properly at the same time.

Surprise may be obtained by the use of speed. Without surprise your opponent will know what type of technique will be applied and he can easily counter it. With surprise any battle may be won, without it all battles will probably be lost.

The student must practice the come alongs in order to become proficient. He must, in fact, continue to practice to maintain his proficiency. If you learn to fly and then don't keep in practice you will soon be unable to fly with any safety. Thus if you omit practicing the come alongs soon you will be unable to apply them with any degree of safety to yourself.

You must have good knowledge for the come along techniques you apply. This can be gained by studying the techniques thoroughly until you completely understand their application and principle.

If the student seriously applies the above elements to his application of a come along he will find he has gained a much higher rate of success with his opponents.

Although the following come alongs are applied when one is facing his opponent, it should be realized that these same techniques may also be applied when a subject is approached from the side or from the rear. In all probability the techniques will be more successful if they are applied as you walk up to your opponent's side.

Extreme caution should be used when practicing come alongs with a partner. When sufficient pressure is applied, your opponent should tap either you, himself or some object such as a wall or floor to let you know it hurts. As soon as you hear or see his tap you must release your pressure. Failure to do this might injure him.

Two Fingers Come Along

Fig. 27

Fig. 28

1. You are standing and facing your opponent (Fig. 27).

2. Grab your opponent's left forefinger and index finger by placing the Yawara Stick on the back of these two fingers, putting your right thumb around these fingers (Fig. 28).

3. Grab with your left hand on your opponent's left wrist and lift his arm up by an upward pull with your left hand. Also apply a backward pressure against your opponent's fingers with your right hand (Fig. 29).

4. An important point to remember about this technique is to make sure your opponent's left arm is straight. This way if he should attempt to kick you, you will be easily able to apply more pressure on his fingers, thus discouraging his kick.

Fig. 29

Four Fingers Come Along

1. Grasp your opponent's left wrist with your left hand (Fig. 30).

2. Pull his hand up toward you, at the same time grasp his four fingers with your right thumb and place the Yawara Stick on the back of his hand (Fig. 31).

3. Apply pressure against his fingers by pushing them back (Fig. 32).

4. It is important, as in the previous technique, to remember to keep his arm straight and high.

Fig. 30

Fig. 31

Fig. 32

5. You may also apply the reverse of this technique when an opponent has his hand on your shoulder (Fig. 33).

6. Grab his left forearm or wrist with your left hand. At the same time grab his fingers by placing your thumb around them and putting your Yawara Stick on the back of his hand (Fig. 34).

7. Now apply pressure downward by bending your opponent's fingers backward and down (Fig. 35).

8. In this reverse technique you need not keep your opponent's arm straight.

Fig. 33

Fig. 34

Fig. 35

Arm Scissors Come Along

1. You are facing your opponent (Fig. 36).

2. You step in with your right foot and strike the back of your opponent's left hand with your right hand. You also place your left hand on your opponent's left shoulder and pull forward slightly (Fig. 37).

3. Pull forward and downward more with your left hand on his left shoulder and at the same time force his left hand into a hammer lock position with your right arm (Fig. 38).

4. Now place the Yawara Stick over your opponent's arm so that it is slightly overlapping; thus it will afford you leverage if you pry up on his arm (Fig. 39).

5. Now grab his collar with your left hand to prevent the subject from rolling out of the technique (Fig. 40).

6. To gain pressure with this come along you need only lift upward with your right arm.

Figs. 36-40

25

Straight Arm Bar Come Along

1. You and your opponent are facing each other (Fig. 41).

2. Grasp your opponent's left wrist with your left hand and step forward, placing your left foot off to your opponent's left side (Fig. 42). You may give a slight pull downward at this time.

3. Pivot on the ball of your left foot so that you are standing beside your opponent, with your right arm over his left arm (Fig. 43). If your opponent should resist you in any way at this time you may easily strike him with the Yawara Stick.

4. Bring your right arm all the way around his left arm and twist his arm with your left hand so that the palm of his hand is facing upward (Fig. 44).

5. Place the Yawara Stick on his forearm with the barb against his arm (Fig. 45). Your right forearm should be either directly under his elbow or slightly up from it.

6. Pressure may be applied by forcing his arm down with your left hand and applying a downward pressure with the Yawara Stick.

Figs. 41-45

27

Neck Come Along

1. This come along is to be applied when coming up to an opponent from the rear (Fig. 46).

2. Turn your hip into your opponent's back. Place your left hand with the thumb side against your opponent's head and pull backward. Now place the Yawara Stick behind the collar bone and apply pressure toward the neck (Fig. 47).

3. This come along is extremely effective for taking a subject short distances. If enough pressure is exerted you can easily lower a man directly to the ground.

Fig. 46

Fig. 47

Barb Come Along

1. You approach your subject from the side (Fig. 48).

2. Grasp your opponent's right wrist with your left hand. At the same time grab your opponent's thumb by lifting your thumb and catching his thumb between your thumb and the Yawara Stick (Fig. 49). Make sure the barb is placed in your opponent's thumb joint.

3. Straighten your opponent's arm by pulling out and down (Fig. 50).

4. Pressure may be exerted by pushing your thumb against his and thus against the barb.

Fig. 48-50

VI

YAWARA STICK ESCAPES

THE ESCAPES demonstrated here are only a few of those which could possibly be used. The reader is encouraged to create new escapes by use of the vital areas which are explained in section IV.

The author has tried to include two escapes, where possible, with each hold. One escape is by using either a vital point or bone edge and the other is by way of a nerve center. The holds used are similar or identical to any the student may find himself in.

Ground fighting has been purposely omitted since it could easily entail a manual equal in size to this one. If caught on the ground you may use the same vital areas that are used when standing.

Wrist Escape No. 1

If a subject should grab the wrist in which you hold your Yawara Stick you should swing your hand toward the palm of his hand (Fig. 51). Twist your hand upward in order to place the barb in the bone on the underside of his arm (Fig. 52). Apply pressure down against the bone edge of his arm (Fig. 53). This is an excellent nerve release technique.

Fig. 51

Fig. 52

Fig. 53

For another escape, you can change the Yawara Stick into your other hand (Fig. 54). Now strike your opponent's elbow with the Yawara Stick (Fig. 55).

Fig. 54

Fig. 55

Wrist Escape No. 2

A subject may grab the hand which is not holding the Yawara Stick (Fig. 56). A simple escape is to strike your opponent's elbow with the Yawara Stick (Fig. 57).

Fig. 56

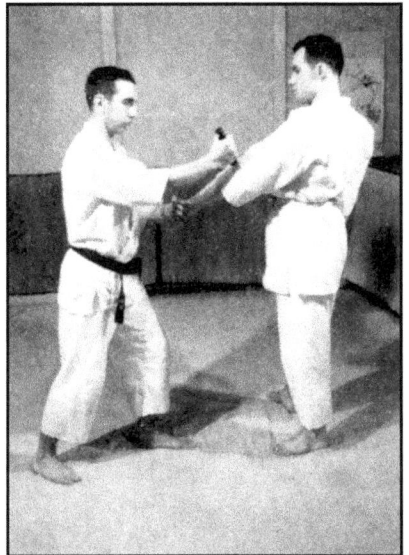

Fig. 57

One Handed Lapel

As a subject grabs you with one hand on your lapel, raise your Yawara Stick up and strike down hard against the back of his hand (Figs. 58, 59 and 60). You can grab his arm with your other hand and twist his arm so as to better expose the back of his hand.

Fig. 58

Fig. 59

Fig. 60

An ideal nerve release from a one handed grab is to place the barb of the Yawara Stick on the bone edge of his wrist and push down (Figs. 61 and 62).

Fig. 61

Fig. 62

Two Handed Lapel

A good nerve release escape when a subject grabs you by both lapels is to place the Yawara Stick in the hollow spot just behind the collarbone and press down (Figs. 63, 64 and 65).

Another method of gaining immediate release is to strike your opponent in the ribs (Fig. 66).

Fig. 63

Fig. 64

Fig. 65

Fig. 66

35

One Hand on Belt

When a subject grabs you on the belt with one hand you may strike him on the muscle in the upper part of his arm (Figs. 67 and 68).

Fig. 67

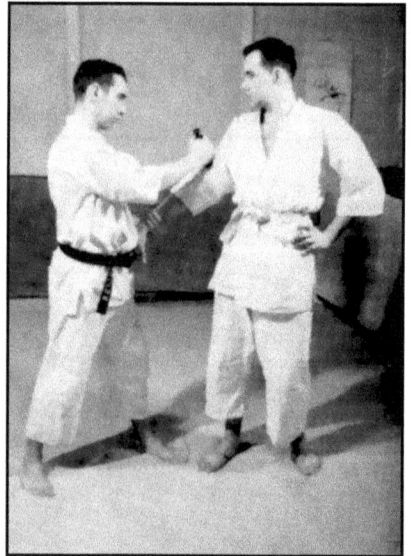

Fig. 68

Two Hands on Belt

A nerve release from being grabbed on the belt by both of your opponent's hands is to place the Yawara Stick in the pit of his throat and push backward (Figs. 69 and 70).

Fig. 69

Fig. 70

A strike against an opponent's temple will also produce a good escape (Fig. 71).

Fig. 71

Front Choke

The front choke, although dangerous to you, is an easy hold to gain release from. When a choke is applied to you, you can easily strike your opponent under the elbow (Figs. 72 and 73).

Fig. 72

Fig. 73

A good nerve release may be produced by placing the barb of the Yawara Stick on your opponent's nose and pushing backward (Fig. 74).

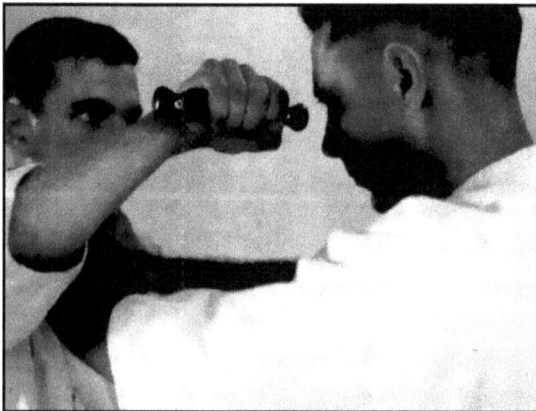

Fig. 74

Rear Choke (Arms Extended)

If an opponent should grab you from the rear in a choke your first move is to step back with your right foot and raise your arm up so that your elbow is above your opponent's arm (Figs. 75, 76 and 77). Now strike downward against your opponent's temple.

Fig. 75

Fig. 76

Fig. 77

Naked Choke

The rear choke is a very dangerous choke to have someone apply on you (Fig. 78). It can cause unconsciousness in a short period of time if properly applied. Your escape should therefore be as rapid as possible. You may easily strike your opponent in the head or the crotch (Figs. 79 and 80).

A nerve release may be effected by placing the barb on your opponent's wrist bone and applying pressure on it (Fig. 81).

Fig. 78

Fig. 79

Fig. 80

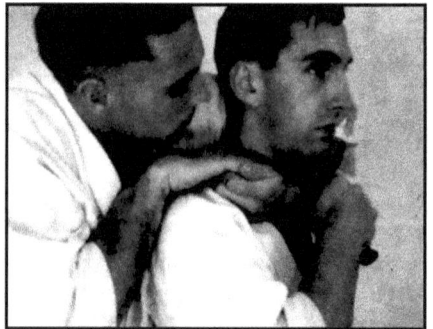

Fig. 81

40

Bear Hug (Over Arms)

To escape from the bear hug you need only strike your opponent in the crotch (Figs. 82 and 83).

Fig. 82

Fig. 83

You may gain another release by placing your Yawara Stick in your opponent's ribs and twisting and pushing against them (Fig. 84).

Fig. 84

41

Bear Hug (Under Arms)

This is a slight variation from the bear hug given above, (Fig. 85).

Fig. 85

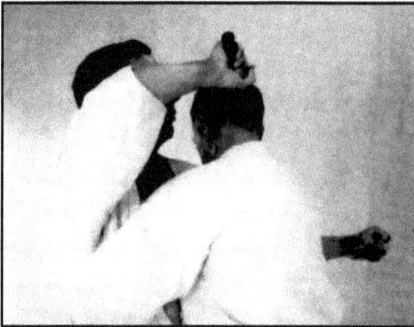

Fig. 86

A strike against the top of the head produces a good escape (Fig. 86).

Fig. 87

You may place the Yawara Stick in the nerve under the ear to attain a good nerve escape (Fig. 87).

Grasp From Behind (Over Arms)

A grasp from behind can be obtained very rapidly and may be quite a surprise to the officer (Fig. 88). An escape may be made by striking your opponent directly in the thigh muscle (Fig. 89).

Fig. 88

Fig. 89

A nerve release may be secured if the Yawara Stick is placed against the inner thigh muscle and pressure is directed backward (Fig. 90).

Fig. 90

Grasp From Behind (Under Arms)

This hold can easily be escaped from by striking your opponent in the head with the Yawara Stick (Figs. 91 and 92).

Fig. 91

Fig. 92

You may easily secure a nerve release by placing the barb against a knuckle of your opponent's hand and applying pressure (Fig. 93).

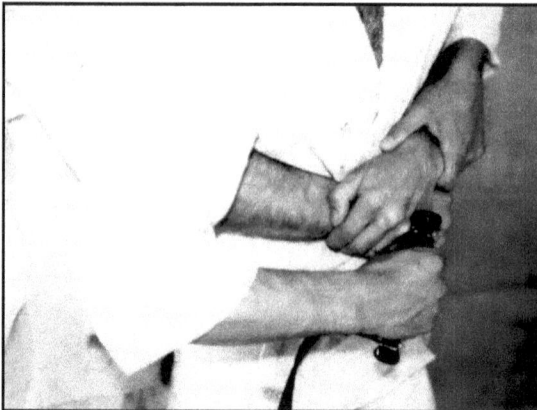
Fig. 93

Hammer Lock

The escape from a hammer lock is to strike your opponent against the head (Figs. 94 and 95).

Fig. 94

Fig. 95

Head Lock

Fig. 96

The head lock is a binding hold and can produce unconsciousness if properly applied (Fig. 96).

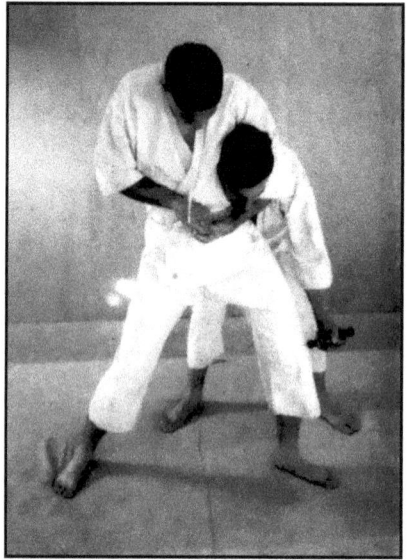

Fig. 97

To escape from this strike the opponent against his knee (Fig. 97).

Fig. 98

An excellent nerve release is gained by placing the Yawara Stick in your opponent's eye and pushing against it (Fig. 98).

46

Full Nelson

An escape may be gained from a full nelson by striking into the stomach (Figs. 99 and 100).

Fig. 99

Fig. 100

A nerve release may be gained by placing the barb on a knuckle and applying pressure (Figure 101).

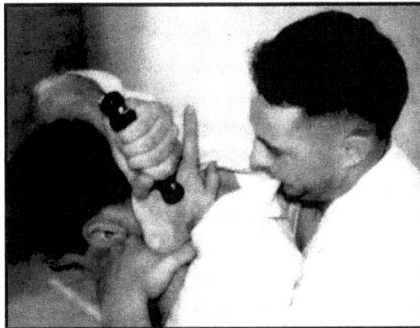
Fig. 101

Running Attack

Fig. 102

When an opponent is making a forward running attack against you, you may secure a victory by striking your opponent on the side of the neck (Fig. 102).

You may also easily strike an opponent on the top of his head (Fig. 103).

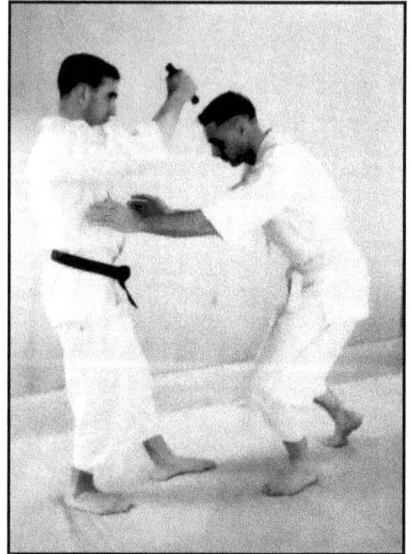

Fig. 103

Two Man Attack (Front and Back)

Fig. 104

When two men are attacking it is extremely important to be very fast in your movements (Fig. 104).

A good escape is to first strike the attacker in front with a blow to the solar plexus (Fig. 105); next, strike the opponent at your rear, on the temple (Fig. 106).

Fig. 105

Fig. 106

Two Man Attack (Right and Left)

Fig. 107

When attacked from the sides you may strike the opponent on your left in the Adam's apple and the opponent on the right in the crotch (Figs. 107, 108 and 109).

Fig. 108

Fig. 109

SECTION TWO
The Police Baton

I

GENERAL

THE SECOND WEAPON to be covered is the police baton. It comes in various sizes and the size used is a matter of individual preference. All of the techniques demonstrated in this section can be employed with nearly any sized baton.

It is not advisable to change baton sizes. If you learn these techniques with a fifteen inch baton then try and stay with it. Other batons may weigh more or less and have different balance.

The baton has a great advantage in that when a subject sees you coming at him with it he can imagine that you are going to hit him with it. Most people cannot defend themselves from a baton and they will, in many instances, give up before engaging in a fight.

The Yawara Stick, on the other hand, doesn't give the appearance of being dangerous so the opposite response will probably be forthcoming. (The subject will try and fight.)

A disadvantage of the baton is that in a lot of situations you must pull the baton back in order to strike. This momentarily leaves you vulnerable to attack and also gives your opponent a forewarning that he will or may be struck.

All of the techniques will be demonstrated while using the baton in the right hand. They are demonstrated in this manner to avoid confusion. The technique can, of course, be applied with either hand. It should also be remembered that the baton can be and is used as an extension of the officer's hand.

II

HOW TO STRIKE WITH THE BATON

THERE HERE ARE THREE BASIC METHODS of striking attacks with the baton—the straight strikes, the ramming strikes and the combination of straight and ramming strikes similar to those used with the Yawara Stick.

In the straight strikes the baton is pulled back and then comes forward and strikes as a club does. You may also use the other end to strike (Figs. 114 and 115). The vital points which are most applicable to these techniques of striking are shown on *Baton Vital Points Diagram IV*. The reaction acquired by the receiving subject is:

Temples: The subject may be stunned by a light blow, knocked out by a fairly heavy blow or killed by a strong blow.

Ears: A concussion may result from a strike here. Deafness may also occur.

Nose: The nose may be broken by a fairly accurate strike upon the bridge. Severe bleeding may ensue if struck properly.

⬚ roat: The throat or Adam's apple may cause temporary loss of consciousness and speech.

Collar Bone: This bone is easy to break if struck rapidly down and forward. When broken the shoulder and arm will become useless.

Elbow: The bone edge at the arm joint (Elbow) may be cracked or broken if struck with sufficient force. The arm will become useless if the elbow is cracked or broken.

Wrist: This area may be struck on either the top or under side (Location of the bone surfaces). A severe strike will break or paralyze the wrist and possibly the hand.

Rib Cage: The area where the ribs are covering the body is all vital. A hard strike may break one or more ribs and cause severe pain.

Kidney: If struck here the subject will experience severe pain and he may be knocked unconscious.

Solar Plexus: The subject may be knocked out if struck here or temporarily put out of commission due to loss of wind.

Crotch: If struck directly in the testicles a man will lose consciousness and/or have severe pain.

Knee: The knee or kneecap may be broken or dislocated if struck on the kneecap or on the sides of the knee where bone surfaces are vulnerable. There are many more vital points than those listed above; however, the author feels that more might be a burden to the student, since, if he tries to learn too many, he may not gain proficiency in any of them.

The student should be careful in using these points except under extreme emergencies. A subject with a weak heart or some other physical problem could easily be killed instead of just injured by striking any of the aforementioned vital points.

The vital points attacked when using the baton in the jabbing or ramming method are the same as those used for the Yawara Stick. The butt end may also be used in these series of techniques. Refer back to diagrams for the Yawara Stick.

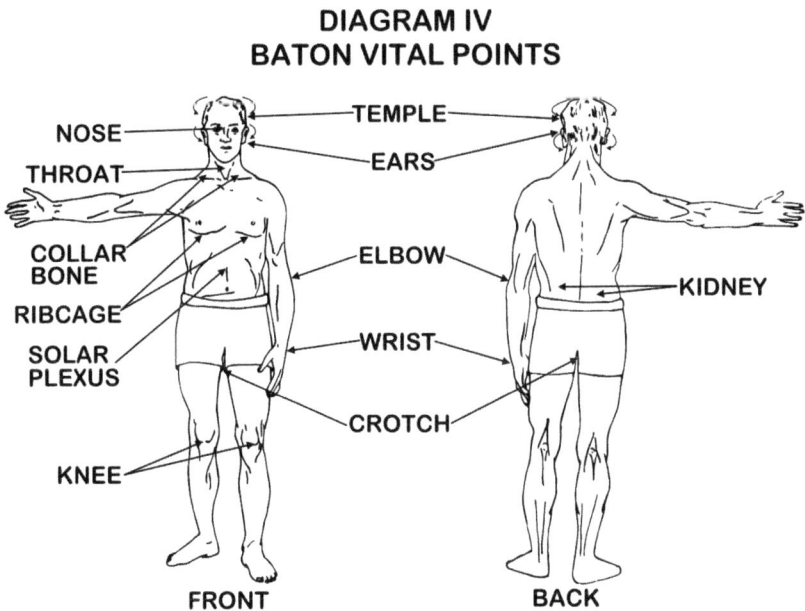

DIAGRAM IV
BATON VITAL POINTS

The following figures will demonstrate the use of the baton strikes:

1. Strike against the nose (straight strike) (Fig. 110).

Fig. 110

2. Strike against the knee (straight strike) (Fig. 111).

Fig. 111

3. Strike against the collar bone (straight strike) (Fig. 112).

Fig. 112

4. Strike against the solar plexus (straight strike) (Fig. 113).

Fig. 113

5. Strike against the temple (butt end) (Fig. 114).

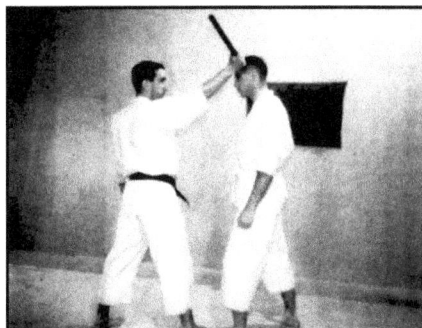

Fig. 114

6. Strike against the ribs (butt end) (Fig. 115).

Fig. 115

7. Strike against the chin (ramming strike) (Fig. 116).

Fig. 116

8. Strike against the solar plexus (ramming strike) (Fig. 117).

Fig. 117

The third method of striking consists of holding the baton in the middle and using it as you would a Yawara Stick. The Yawara Stick diagrams should also be referred to for these points.

1. Strike against the temple (Fig. 118).

Fig. 118

2. Strike against the kidney (Fig. 119).

Fig. 119

III

GENERAL BATON DEFENSES

THE OPPONENT who wrestles would pose no problem if he is struck in the following manner(s) before he has a chance to grab the officer. Once the officer is grabbed he must merely strike vital points similar to the escapes used in the last chapter of this second section. The following photos will help to illustrate some of the areas which can be attacked.

1. Strike the kidney (straight strike) (Fig. 120).

Fig. 120

2. Strike the chin (Yawara Stick style) (Fig. 121).

Fig. 121

3. Strike the throat (ramming strike) (Fig. 122).

Fig. 122

4. Strike the ribs (straight strike) (Fig. 123).

Fig. 123

5. Strike the temple (ramming strike) (Fig. 124).

Fig. 124

An attack from a boxer may be dealt with very efficiently. In fighting against a boxer it is best to try and use bone edges for striking, e.g. elbows, wrists, temples, etc. Vital points should be considered next. The following photos will help to illustrate this point.

1. Strike the fist (straight strike) (Fig. 125).

Fig. 125

2. Strike the wrist (straight strike) (Fig. 126).

Fig. 126

3. Strike the elbow (straight strike) (Fig. 127).

Fig. 127

4. Strike the knee (straight strike) (Fig. 128).

Fig. 128

5. Strike the throat (ramming strike) (Fig. 129).

Fig. 129

6. Strike the solar plexus (ramming strike) (Fig. 130).

Fig. 130

The knife fighter poses a grave problem to the unarmed man. When armed with a baton the problem should not be a large one.

One thing to remember is to be unafraid of his knife. He has more reason to be frightened of you armed with the baton. Remember you probably have the advantage over him even if you are not trained.

The following photos will serve as a guide to some of the vital points to attack against a knife fighter. If possible strike at the knife and try to knock it out of the opponent's hand, then follow through.

1. Strike the knife (straight strike) (Figs. 131 and 132).

Fig. 131

Fig. 132

2. Strike the wrist (straight strike) (Fig. 133).

Fig. 133

3. Strike the temple (straight strike) (Fig. 134).

4. Strike the elbow (straight strike) (Fig. 135).

Fig. 135

5. Strike the collar bone (straight strike) (Fig. 136).

Fig. 136

65

V

BATON COME ALONGS

As in the other COME ALONGS AND HOLDS the subject with whom the officer practices must tap when sufficient pressure has been applied. As a subject you should not attempt to resist the application of the come along. If continual resistance in practice is applied, then the technique(s) cannot be properly learned. Always remember to practice come alongs and holds with care.

The Crotch Come Along

This technique is applied when the officer approaches his subject from the rear.

1. The baton is grasped in the middle (Fig. 137).

2. As the baton is placed between the legs the officer should grasp the subject by the back of the collar (Fig. 138).

Fig. 137

Fig. 138

3. The officer should lower the subject by the back of his collar and by pulling his hand (with the baton in it) back toward himself (Fig. 139).

4. If the subject resists and is very belligerent the officer may drive him into a wall (Fig. 140).

Fig. 139

Fig. 140

The Arm Bar Come Along

1. This technique may be applied when coming up to a subject from the front, side or rear. For convenience it will be demonstrated here when the opponent is approached from the front (Fig. 141).

2. Holding the baton in your right hand advance your left foot forward and grab the subject's left wrist with your left hand (Fig. 142).

Fig. 141

Fig. 142

3. Pivot to your rear and your subject's left side (Fig. 143).

4. Place your baton under his elbow and support it on your arm (Fig. 144).

5. Apply continuous pressure downward with your left hand. Be sure his wrist is twisted so that the palm is facing up

Fig. 143

Fig. 144

The Choke Come Alongs

On all choke come alongs pressure should be applied gradually. Loss of consciousness and possible death can result if pressure is applied too forcefully. For best results all of these chokes should be applied when approaching a subject from the rear.

Choke One Come Along

1. Grasp your baton with your right hand (Fig. 145).

Fig. 145

2. Simultaneously place your hand on the subject's left shoulder and the baton across his throat
(Fig. 146).

Fig. 146

3. Grab the other end of the baton with your left hand and spread your elbows apart
(Fig. 147).

Fig. 147

69

Choke Two Come Along

1. Hold the baton as you normally do but turn your wrist so that the palm is facing upward
(Fig. 148).

Fig. 148

2. Simultaneously place your hand on the subject's left shoulder and the baton across his throat
(Fig. 149).

Fig. 149

3. With your left hand grab the other end of the baton and apply pressure by gradually separating your elbows
(Fig. 150).

Fig. 150

Choke Three Come Along

1. Hold the baton by the end in your left hand
(Fig. 151).

Fig. 151

2. Simultaneously place your left hand on your opponent's left shoulder and the baton across his throat
(Fig. 152).

Fig. 152

3. Grasp the other end of the baton with your right hand and apply pressure back and down gradually
(Fig. 153).

Fig. 153

V

MISCELLANEOUS BATON ESCAPES

ONLY A FEW ESCAPEs will be demonstrated here. The officer who has read the first part of this book will be able to figure out escapes from all holds where the baton hand and arm are free. Where the baton hand or arm is captured the officer is advised to consult *Police Ju Jitsu*, published in 1962.

For an escape from a head lock strike your opponent's knee with the baton (Fig. 154).

Fig. 154

Fig. 155

From a full nelson an escape is to strike your opponent's left elbow (Fig. 155).

If held in a front choke you may strike your opponent in the ribs (Fig. 156).

Fig. 156

When an opponent holds you in a rear choke you may step backward with your right foot and strike against the inside of your opponent's left knee (Figs. 157 and 158).

Fig. 157

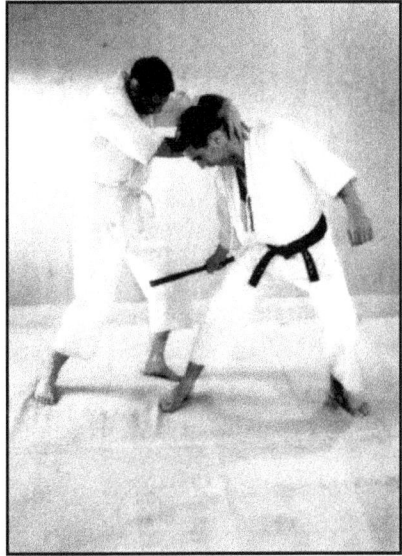

Fig. 158

If an opponent should grab you from behind you may strike him on the right knee (Fig. 159).

Fig. 159

Fig. 160

The opponent who grabs you from the front may be defended against by striking him in the temple with the butt of the baton (Fig. 160).

For the opponent who grabs your arm with both of his hands the strike on the elbow is a sure escape
(Fig. 161).

74

Fig. 161

9 781961 301498